# I Love
# Triceratops,
# T rex,
# Stegosaurus,
## and other
# dinosaurs

### Stegosaurus
#### (STEG-owe-SORE-uss)

- lived around 155-144 million years ago
- 13 ft (4 m) tall

This box shows you how to pronounce the dinosaur's name. It also shows you how big the dinosaur was and tells you when it lived.

 This is the symbol for a meat-eating dinosaur.

This is the symbol for a plant-eating dinosaur.

Dinosaur experts learn more about dinosaurs every day. Although we cannot include future discoveries, we have tried to ensure that this book is as accurate as possible.

Castle Street PRESS

# Tyrannosaurus rex

**Tyrannosaurus rex** was a fierce **meat eater**. It could crunch bones in its strong **jaw** and even swallow its food whole!

## Little arms

**T rex** had such short **arms** that it couldn't even touch its nose!

sharp teeth..........

jaw closed

short arm

# Mad about T rex

T rex had a bite that was six times stronger than that of a lion!

A hungry T rex could chomp its way through the equivalent of 1,500 sausages a day!

T rex was so large, it could be as tall as a double-decker bus!

It took gigantic steps that were as long as a small car.

jaw

tail

## Tyrannosaurus rex
(tie-RAN-owe-SORE-uss-REX)

- lived around 67-65 million years ago
- 13 ft (4 m) tall

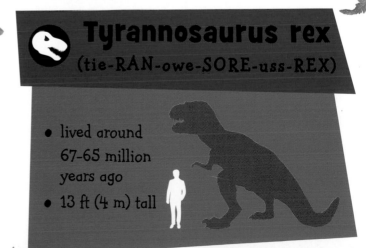

# Parasaurolophus

**Parasaurolophus** had a long **crest** that stuck out from its head like a **snorkel**! It would walk on all fours when it was eating, but would switch to two legs when it needed a quick escape.

tail

long back leg

foot

crest

# Mad about parasaurolophus

Parasaurolophus had side teeth, but no teeth in the front of its mouth. As teeth wore out, new ones grew to replace them.

The crest on its head could grow up to 6 ft (1.8 m) long!

## Hooting horn

**Parasaurolophus**'s long crest was actually a hollow, bony **horn** that it may have used to make loud, **hooting sounds**.

head

## Parasaurolophus
(par-a-SORE-ow-LOAF-uss)

- lived around 76–74 million years ago
- 16 ft (4.9 m) tall

# Brachiosaurus

**Brachiosaurus** was a giant eating machine! Its **arms** were longer than its **back legs**, so its body sloped down towards its tail. Like other dinosaurs, even the huge **brachiosaurus** hatched from an egg.

**Brachiosaurus**
(BRACH-ee-owe-SORE-uss)

- lived around 155–140 million years ago
- 42 ft (13 m) tall

tail......

## Giant dinosaurs

**Apatosaurus** (brontosaurus) also had a long neck and tail like **brachiosaurus**.

back leg

# Taller than T rex

**Brachiosaurus** could raise its head up to 42 ft (13 m) off the ground—that's over twice the height of **T rex**.

long neck

arm

## Mad about brachiosaurus

Brachiosaurus was one of the heaviest dinosaurs. It could weigh over 70 tons (63,500 kg), or more than 30 cars!

Its neck was twice as long as a giraffe's!

Brachiosaurus had scary, chisel-like teeth, but fortunately it only ate plants.

It was a big eater, eating up to 440 lb (200 kg) of food a day. That's like eating 200 cabbages!

# Allosaurus

**Allosaurus** was a terrifying **meat eater** that existed way before T rex. It had a massive **jaw** and **sharp claws** on its three-fingered hands.

## Mad about allosaurus

Allosaurus could open its mouth wide enough to swallow an adult pig in one gulp.

Its short arms ended in daggerlike claws. Allosaurus used these claws to tear up its victims.

It had two horns that shaded its eyes from the sun—like a pair of sunglasses!

sharp claw

**tail**

## Shapely teeth

**Allosaurus** had about 40 long, sharp **teeth** with **sawlike** edges. Its teeth curved backwards to stop its victims from escaping.

**teeth**

### Allosaurus
(al-oh-SORE-uss)

- lived around 153-135 million years ago
- 20 ft (6 m) tall

# Spinosaurus

**Spinosaurus** was one of the largest **meat-eating** dinosaurs ever—even bigger than **T rex**. With massive **spines** sticking out of its back, it looked terrifying!

### 🦖 Spinosaurus
(SPY-no-SORE-uss)

- lived around 125-95 million years ago
- 18.5 ft (5.6 m) tall

spines

tail

# Mad about spinosaurus

Spinosaurus had a long crocodile-like snout that was great for catching and eating fish.

The bony spines on its back could be as tall as 6 ft (2 m). That's taller than most adults!

## Warm up!

The **spines** on **spinosaurus**'s back were called a "**sail**." When the sail turned towards the sun, it helped spinosaurus to **warm up** quickly.

sail

crocodile-like snout

# Stegosaurus

**Stegosaurus** had large, tough **plates** on its back and sharp **spikes** on its tail. The spikes helped protect it from attackers.

head...........

### Stegosaurus
### (STEG-owe-SORE-uss)

- lived around 155–144 million years ago
- 13 ft (4 m) tall

plate

foot

plate

## Mad about stegosaurus

Some scientists think stegosaurus used its plates to impress other stegosauruses— the big show-off!

As it chewed, stegosaurus stored food in its cheeks like a hamster.

Although its brain was tiny, some scientists think stegosaurus had another brain in its tail!

spike......

leg

## Tiny brain

**Stegosaurus** was the size of a bus, but its brain was only the size of a walnut.

Its brain would be in here

# Triceratops

Triceratops was a strong, **plant-eating** dinosaur with three **horns** and a bony **frill** on its head. Its sharp horns looked fierce but it probably used them to show off to other dinosaurs.

tail

## Birdlike beak

**Triceratops** had a mouth shaped like a bird's **beak**. It used this to pluck out food.

beak

frill

# Mad about triceratops

Triceratops could weigh as much as two big elephants.

Its huge head was filled with up to 800 sharp teeth! An average human only has 32!

Triceratops means "three-horned face."

horn

**Triceratops**
(try-SERRA-tops)

- lived around 68–65 million years ago
- 10 ft (3 m) tall

# Velociraptor

**Velociraptor** was armed with a terrifying, **sharp claw** on the second toe of each **foot**. Scientists think that **velociraptor** used its claws to grab hold of its victims and climb over them.

## Velociraptor
(vel-O-si-RAP-tor)

- lived around 84-80 million years ago
- 1.6 ft (0.5 m) tall

strong leg

tail

sharp claw

## Toothy jaw

**Velociraptor** had a narrow **jaw** with about 80 sharp, pointed **teeth**. It used the teeth to tear into just about anything.

## Mad about velociraptors

Velociraptor was super speedy. Over short distances, it could run as fast as an Olympic sprinter!

The sharp claws on velociraptor's feet were nearly 2.5 in (6.5 cm) long. That's over half the width of this page!

Velociraptors were smart dinosaurs, hunting for their prey in groups.

Scientists think that velociraptor may have been covered with hair and feathers.

narrow jaw

sharp teeth

# Dino hunt!

**Search the scene. Try to find . . .**

**3** T Rex

**1** Brachiosaurus

**2** Stegosaurus

**4** Allosaurus

**2** Spinosaurus

**6** dinosaur bones

# Guess who?

Look at the pictures, read the clues, and guess the dinosaurs!

**1**

I have a big, spiny "sail" sticking out of my back.

**2**

I'm as big as a bus, but my brain is only the size of a walnut.

**3**

I have three horns and a big, bony frill on my head. I eat plants.

**4**

I am very heavy and my neck is twice as long as a giraffe's.

**5**

I use my long, bony crest to make loud, hooting sounds.

**6**

I have a large, curved claw on the second toe of each foot.